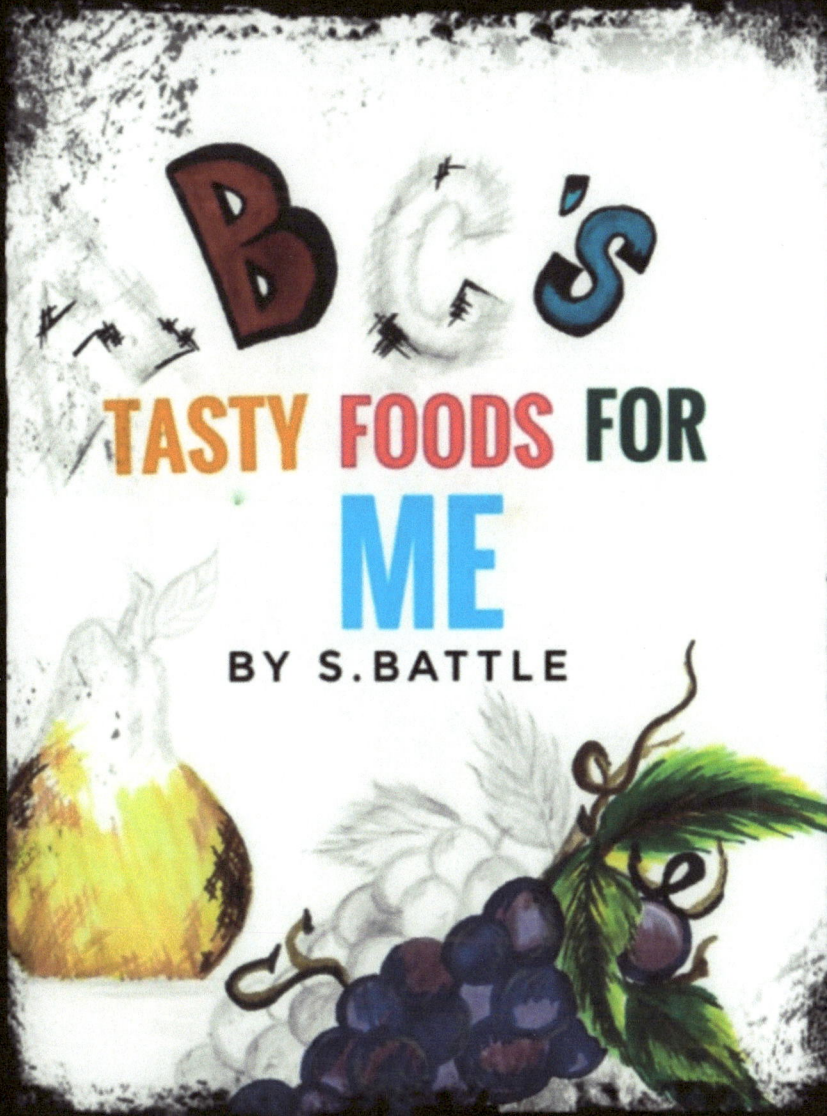

ABC's
TASTY FOODS FOR ME
BY S.BATTLE

ALPHABET BOOK

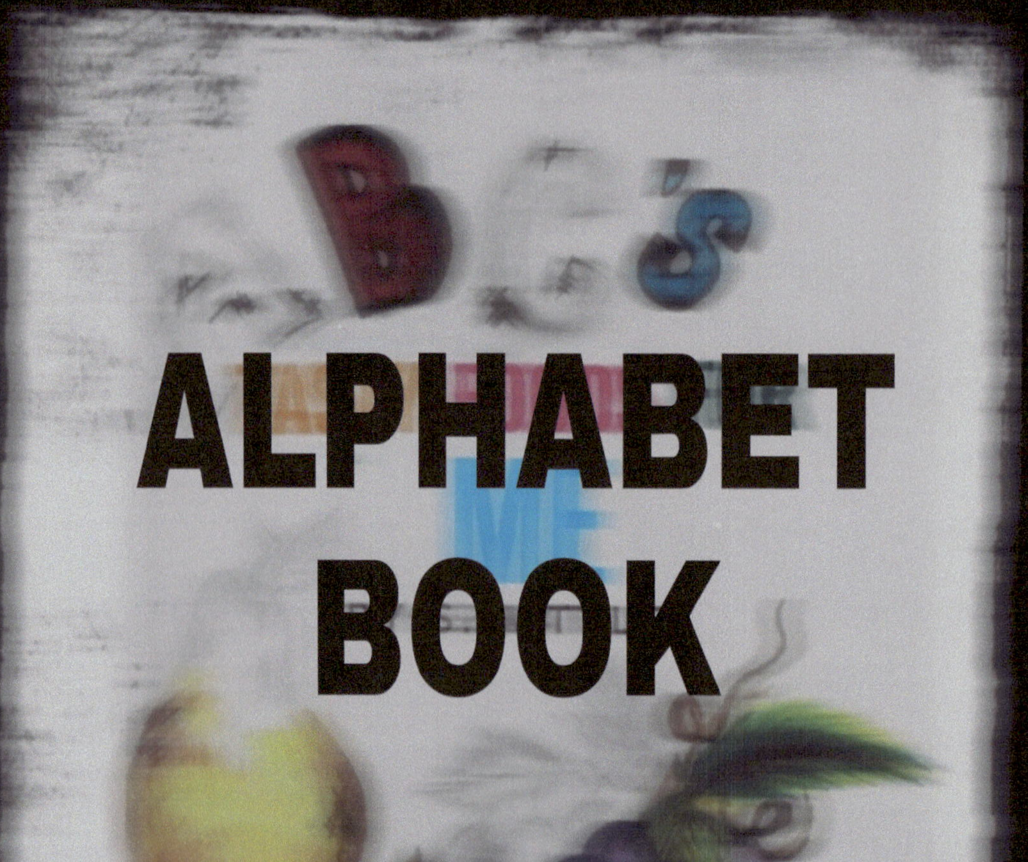

For everyone that refuses to quit

S. Battle

Love Cupcake

FOR EVERYONE THAT REFUSES TO QUIT

FOR EVERYONE THAT REFUSES TO QUIT

FOR EVERYONE THAT REFUSES TO QUIT

FOR EVERYONE THAT REFUSES TO QUIT

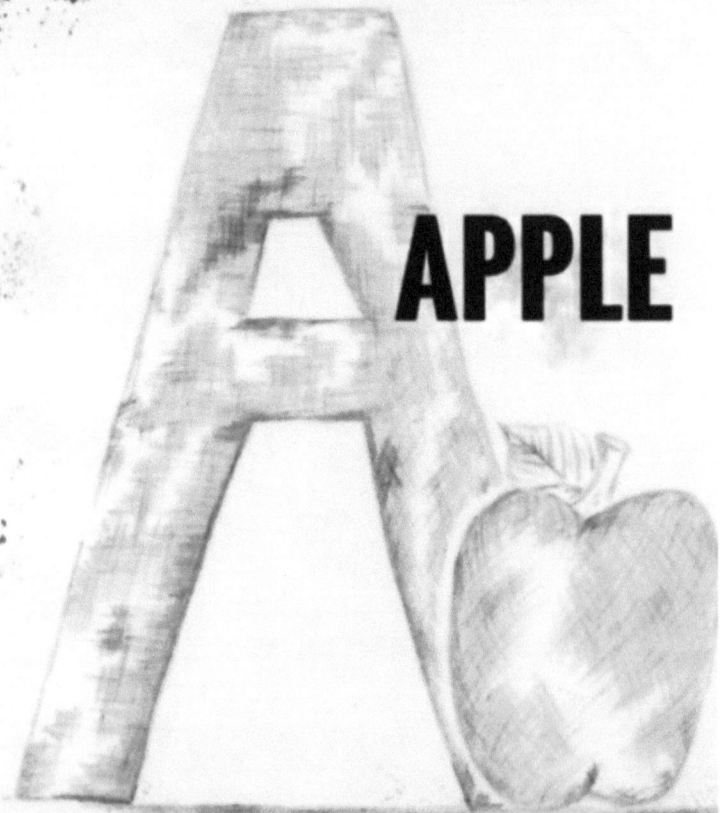

A IS FOR APPLE

APPLE

A IS FOR APPLE

a is for apple

apple

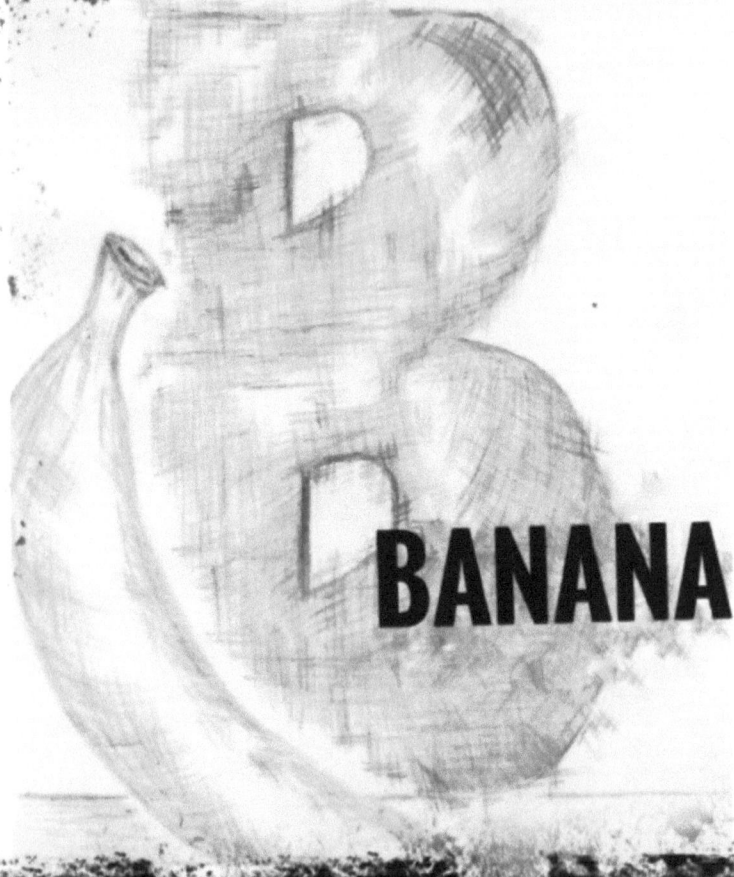

B IS FOR BANANA

BANANA

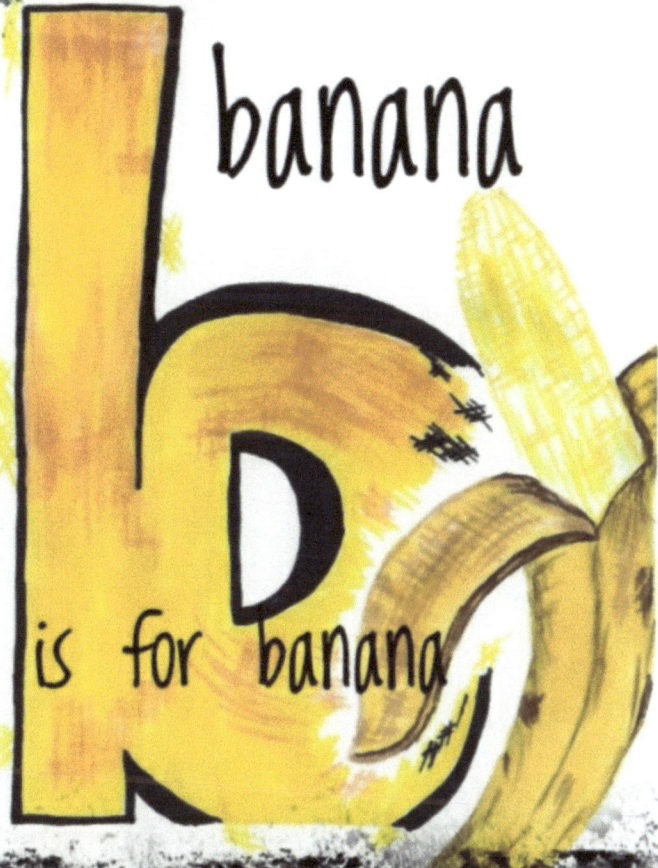

banana

b is for banana

C IS FOR CUPCAKE

CUPCAKE

C is for Cupcake

Cupcake

C

DRAGON FRUIT

D IS FOR DRAGON FRUIT

d is for dragon fruit

dragon fruit

e is for eggplant

eggplant

FRENCH TOAST

F IS FOR FRENCH TOAST

f is for french toast

french toast

g is for grapes

grapes

HAMBURGER

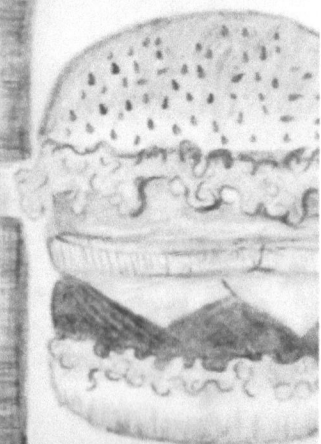

H IS FOR HAMBURGER

h is for hamburger

hamburger

ICE CREAM

I IS FOR ICE CREAM

ice cream

i is for ice cream

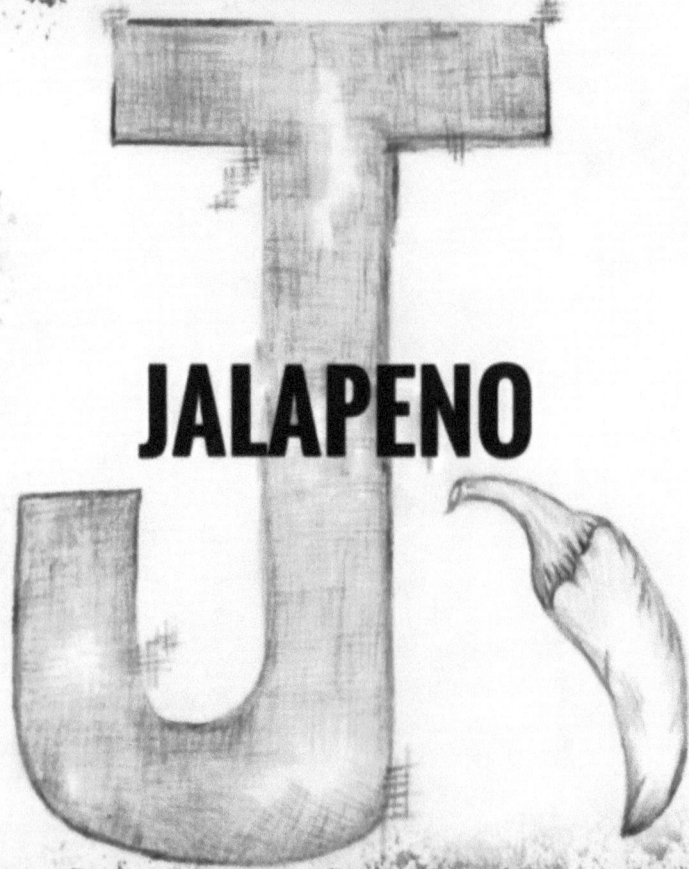

J IS FOR JALAPENO

JALAPENO

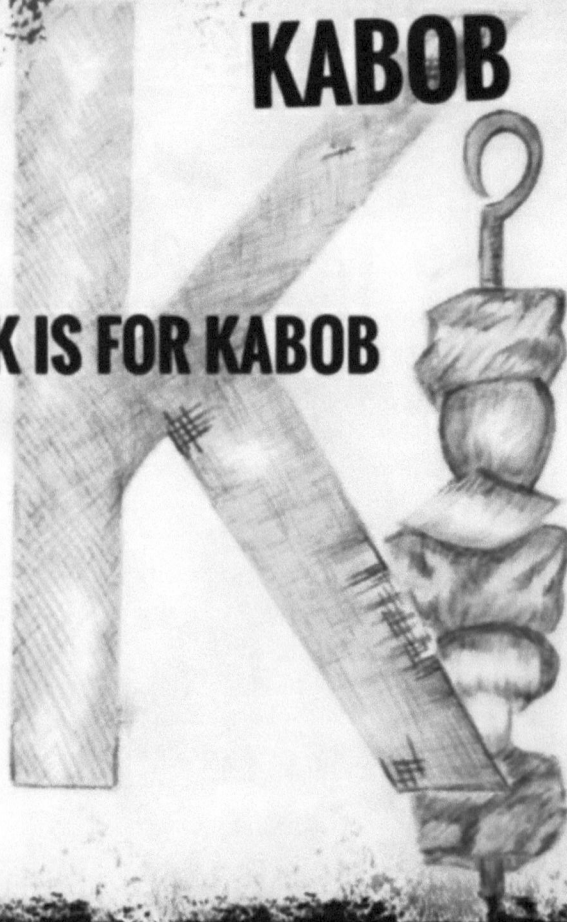

KABOB

K IS FOR KABOB

kabobs

k

k is for kabob

L IS FOR LEMON

LEMON

l is for lemons

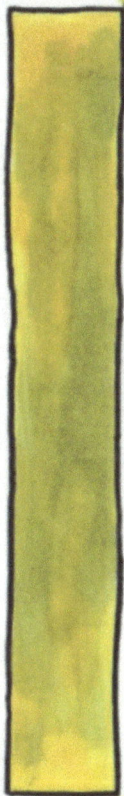 lemons

MILKSHAKE

M IS FOR MILKSHAKE

m is for milkshake

milkshake

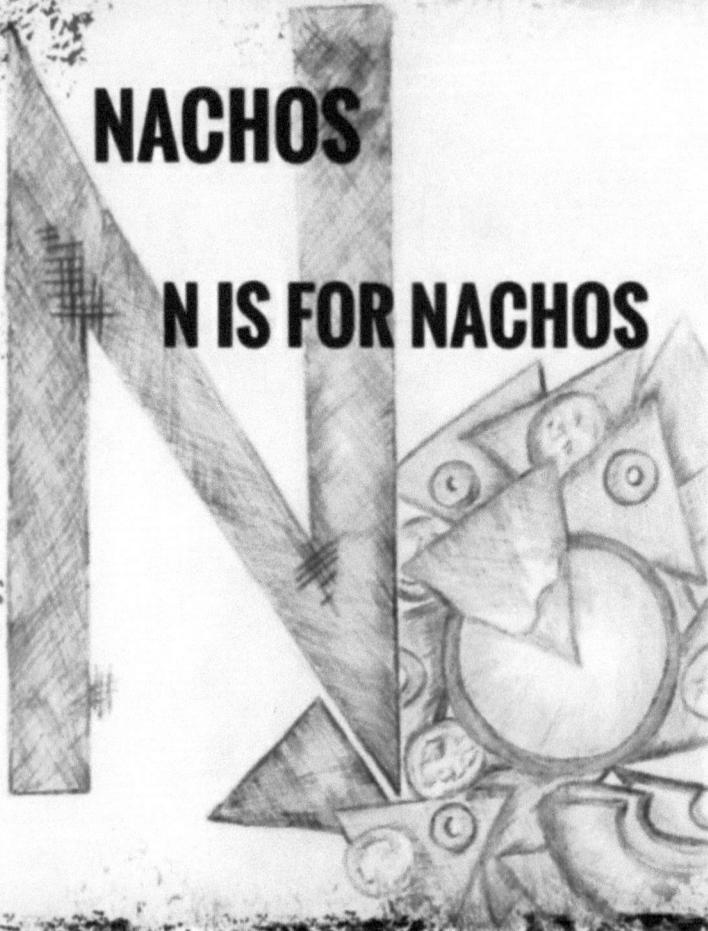

NACHOS

N IS FOR NACHOS

n is for nachos
nachos

ORANGE

O IS FOR ORANGE

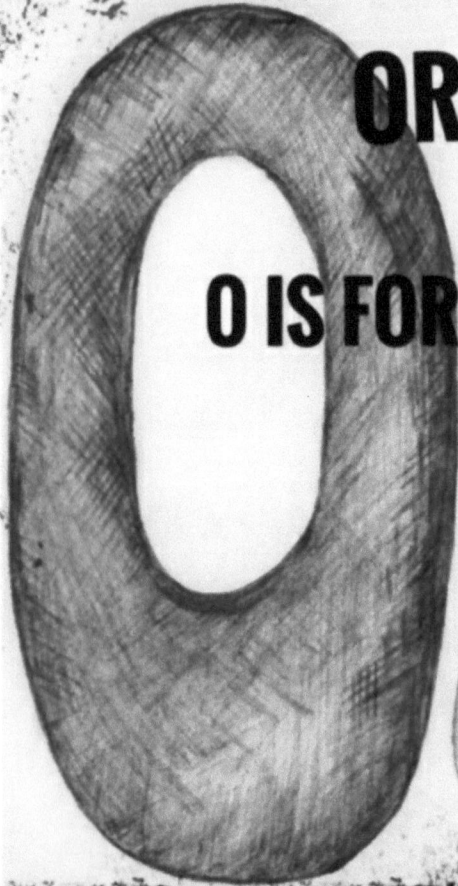

oranges

o is for oranges

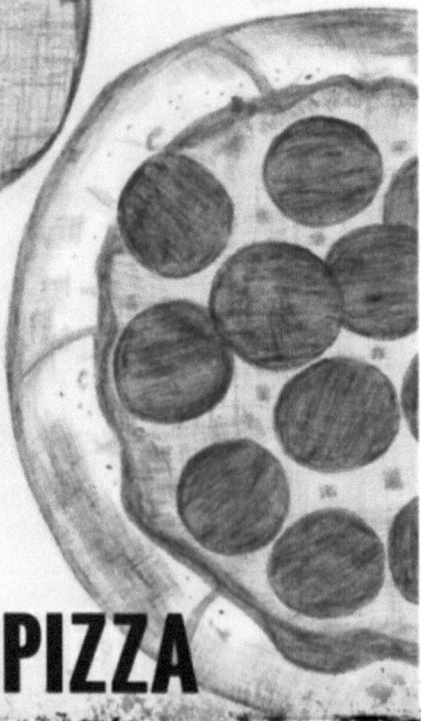

PIZZA

P IS FOR PIZZA

p is for pizza

pizza

P

QUINCE

Q IS FOR QUINCE

quince

q is for quince

RAVIOLI

R IS FOR RAVIOLI

r is for ravioli

ravioli

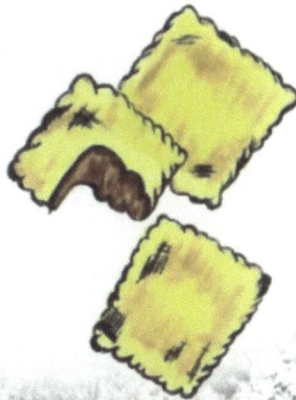

S IS FOR STRAWBERRIES

strawberries

S

s is for strawberries

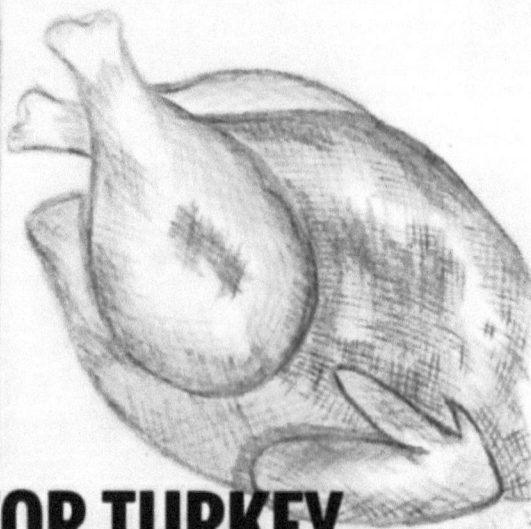

TURKEY

T IS FOR TURKEY

turkey

t is for turkey

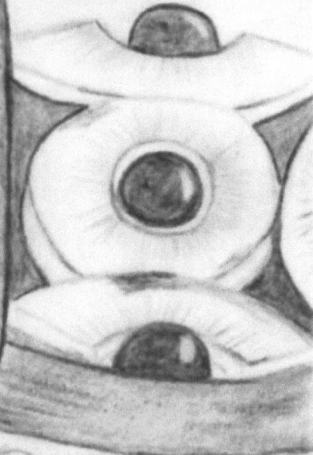

UPSIDE-DOWN
PINEAPPLE
CAKE

U IS FOR
UPSIDE-DOWN
PINEAPPLE CAKE

upside-down
pineapple
cake

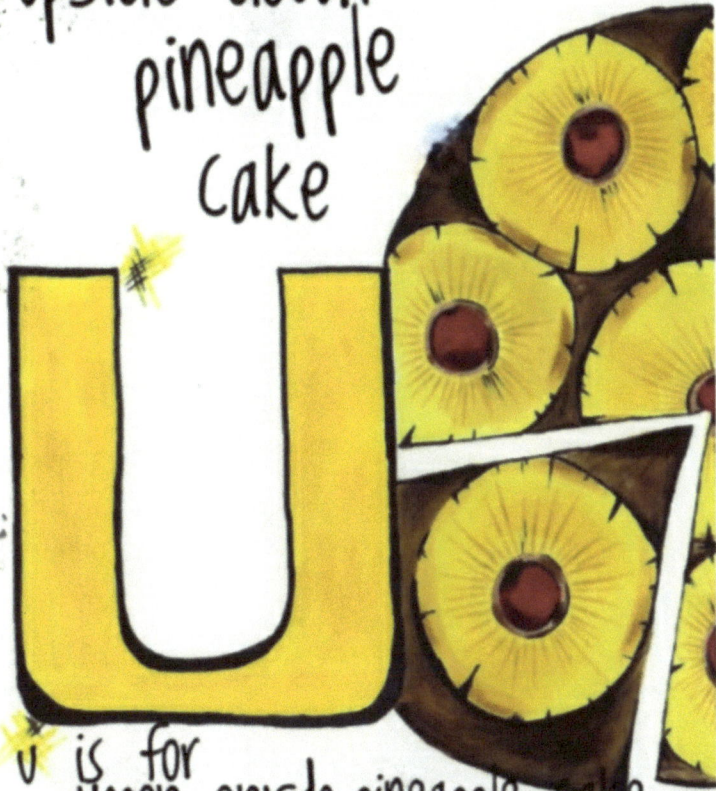

U

is for

umop-apisdn pineapple cake

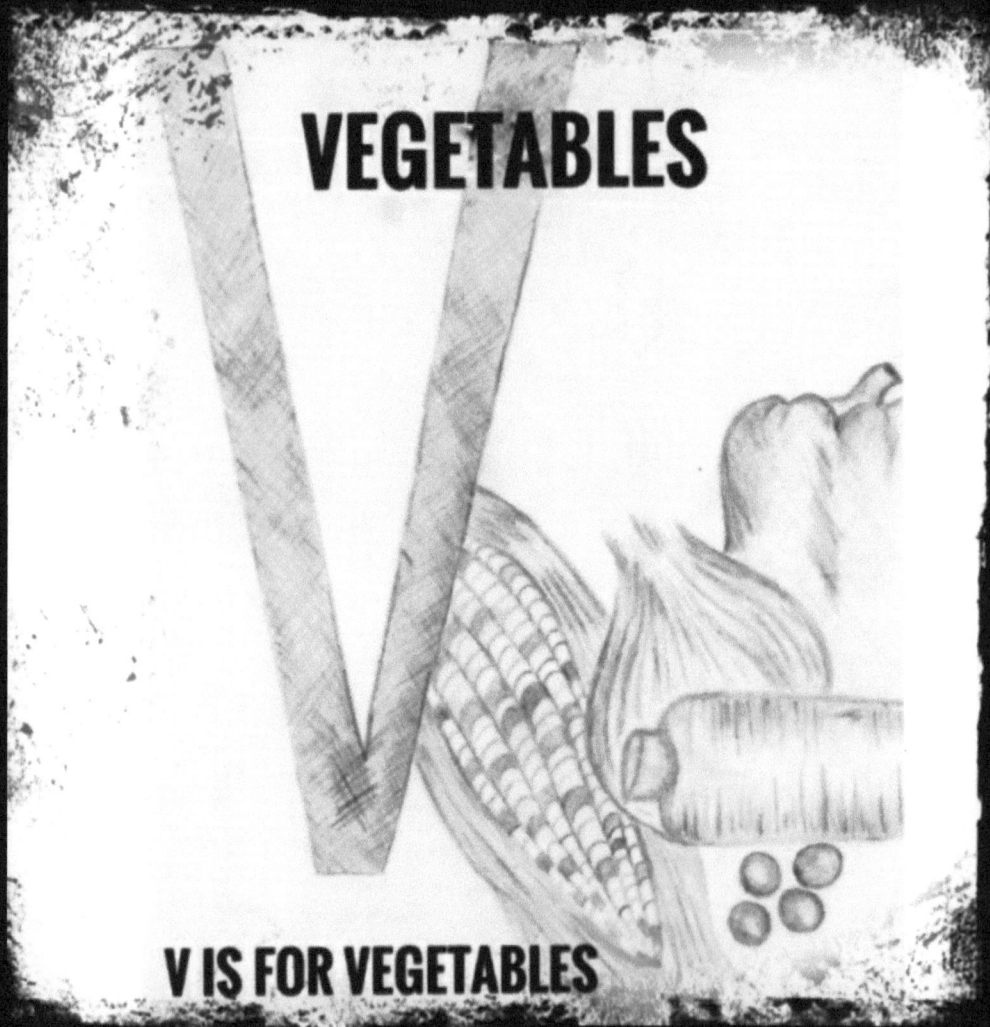

VEGETABLES

V IS FOR VEGETABLES

V is for vegetables

vegetables

VEGETABLE SOUP

green bell pepper

CORN

V onion

peas

CARROT

WATERMELON

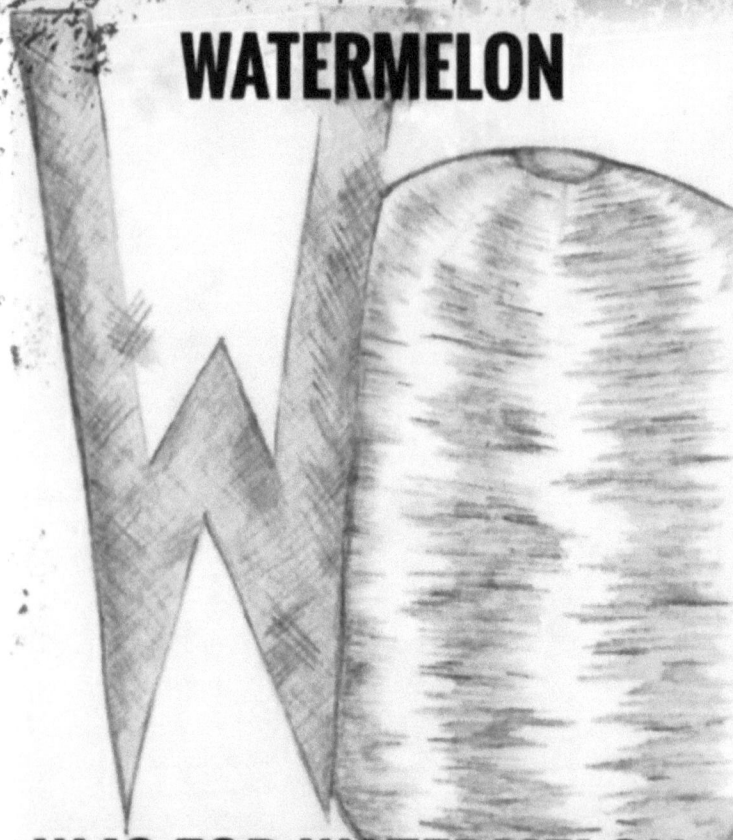

W IS FOR WATERMELON

watermelon

w is for watermelon

XIMENIA

X IS FOR XIMENIA

X is for Ximenia

Ximenia

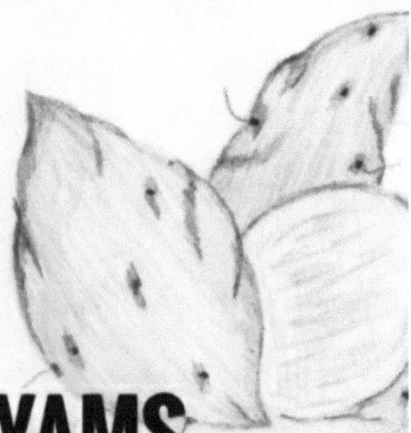

YAMS

Y IS FOR YAMS

y is for yams

yams

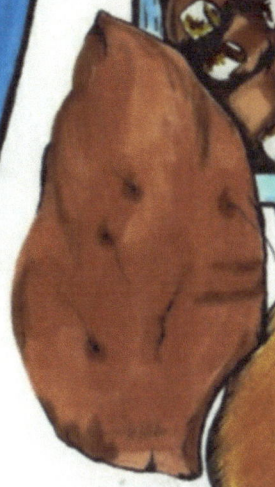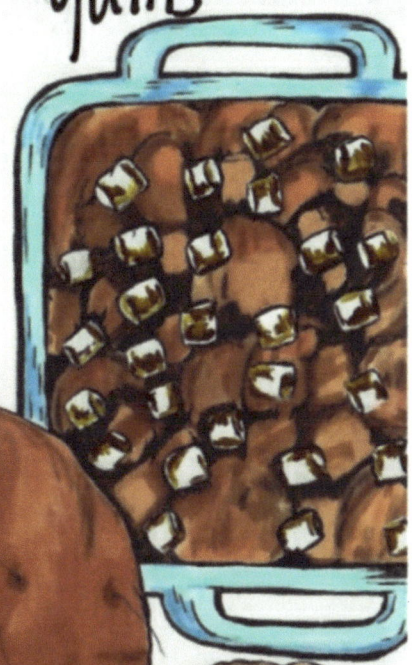

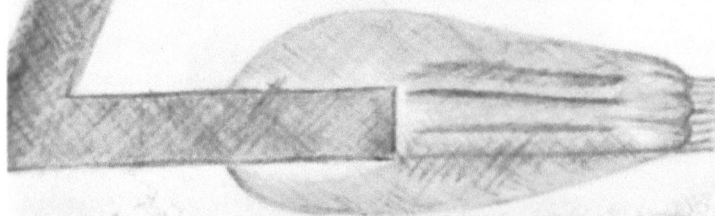

ZUCCHINI

Z IS FOR ZUCCHINI

zucchini

Z is for zucchini

May all your days be sweet

Love Always

C

UPCAKE

CupCake

www.ingramcontent.com/pod-product-compliance
Lightning Source LLC
Chambersburg PA
CBHW042006100426

42736CB00038B/62